Oh Baby!

a little handbook for new moms

© 2011 by Barbour Publishing, Inc.

ISBN 978-1-61626-291-4

Compiled by Elece Hollis in association with Snapdragon Group™, Tulsa, OK.

Cover and interior design: Thinkpen Design

Published by Barbour Publishing, Inc., P.O. Box 719, Uhrichsville, Ohio 44683, www.barbourbooks.com

Our mission is to publish and distribute inspirational products offering exceptional value and biblical encouragement to the masses.

 Member of the
Evangelical Christian
Publishers Association

Printed in China.

a little

handbook

for new

moms

Oh Baby!

BARBOUR
PUBLISHING

It sometimes happens, even in the best of families, that a baby is born. This is not necessarily cause for alarm. The important thing is to keep your wits about you and borrow some money.

ELINOR GOULDING SMITH

Bringing an infant home from the hospital, along with luggage, bags, and flowers from well-wishers, gives a shocking glimpse into the packing problem future outings with baby will necessitate.

There is no finer pleasure
than that of holding and
gazing at a little person
you have carried inside
your belly (and heart)
for nine months.

Taking care of a
newborn is as simple
as assembling a
grand piano
without instructions.

Patience is not a prerequisite
for motherhood, but it should
be the result.

Babies are a handful
and a heart full.

A baby changes you forever,
and keeps you "changing" forever.
Changing diapers, changing clothes,
changing your schedule,
and changing tactics.

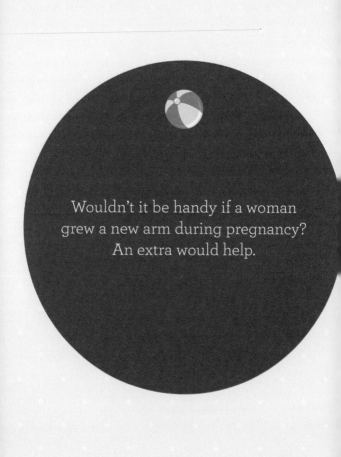

Wouldn't it be handy if a woman grew a new arm during pregnancy? An extra would help.

Don't worry about losing weight after the baby arrives. Initially, you have no time to eat. Later, you have to share every bite!

When you say hello
to your first child,
you are already
outnumbered.

A baby's in the house.
Now it's no longer yours!

Always end the name of your child with a vowel, so that when you yell, the name will carry.

BILL COSBY

New moms may attempt
not to talk in "coos" and
"goo-goos," but it seems
the perfect language.

There is nothing as
exhilarating as playing
peek-a-boo with a
baby at 2 a.m.

Babies are messy,
but their personalities
make up for it.

Why is fat on a baby so adorable, when it is so unsightly on an adult?

Living with a new baby
is as close to living on
an uncharted island as
it comes!

No one has more advice
about the new addition
than Grandma.

Carrying a baby to church for the first time is like arriving at prom in your finest dress with a fancy hairdo and flowers.

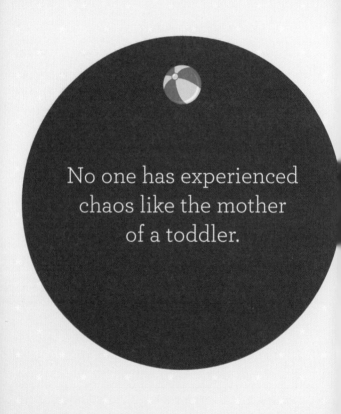

No one has experienced chaos like the mother of a toddler.

When you give out,
don't give up.
Just go take a nap.

Every good and perfect gift is from above, coming down from the Father of the heavenly lights, who does not change like shifting shadows.

JAMES 1:17 NIV

You spend the first year teaching your baby to talk and the rest of his life trying to get him to hush.

How grand it would be to be as popular as a newborn.

Packing to take an
outing with baby can be
like a cross-country move.

A baby's breath is so sweet a flower is named after it.

If you bend down to help a toddler
walk, you will see things from his
perspective—below knee level.

Mamas who have to mop up
mud and bleach out grass
stains have happy children.

A child's smile can make
his mother's heart sing.

A newborn stretches
his mother's heart.
Love doesn't divide—
it multiplies.

Babies are vain. Some can pose for
a camera minutes after birth!

Babies are such a nice
way to start people.

DON HEROLD

Share the wealth—
let others hold your new baby.

Wearing black? Forget about it!
(At least for the next few years.)

A baby gives back
everything you invest in
him—every drop...
literally.

A baby is an alarm clock
with a "snooze control"
gone haywire.

Always remember to be certain
you can recall what you forgot
before you were this tired!

Mamas rock their new babies so much because they need the rest.

No one can teach you
patience or endurance
like an infant.

Sweet toes, poufy hair,
and tiny nose—all these make up
for the diaper thing.

Baby talk joyously
turns intelligent adults
into babblers.

Surely I have calmed and quieted my soul, like a weaned child with his mother; like a weaned child is my soul within me.

PSALM 131:2 NKJV

How can anyone so
small and dear generate
so much laundry?

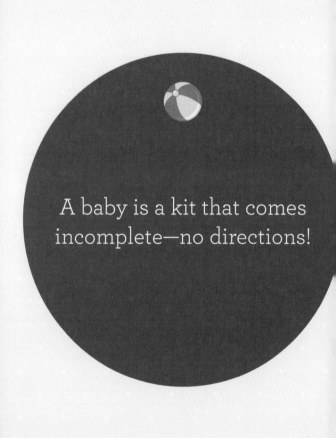

A baby is a kit that comes incomplete—no directions!

Never go to bed without
first peeking at those tiny
toes. It's time well spent!

When your baby is wailing
like a siren, remember how
quiet and heavy he was
while you carried him inside.

What your own mother
was unable to teach you,
your first child will.

There is nothing so
heart-melting as a first smile.
(And no, it wasn't gas.)

The face of a baby
is a beautiful sight
to her mother.

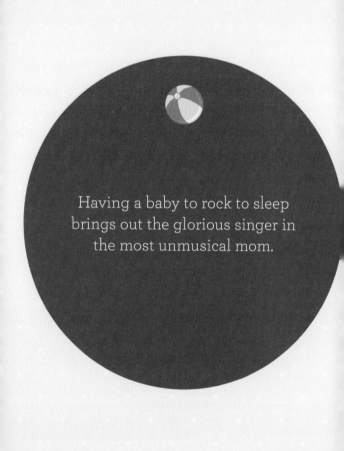

Having a baby to rock to sleep brings out the glorious singer in the most unmusical mom.

The chair in which you sit
with a contented baby in
your lap is decidedly the
best seat in the house.

If you were to open up a baby's head—and I am not for a moment suggesting that you should— you would find nothing but an enormous drool gland.

DAVE BARRY

The skin on the back of an infant's head was God's magnum opus of smells. You can find no more wonderful scent in all creation.

A baby is not a burden.
The true burden is
having nothing to carry.

"Rock-a-bye baby in the treetop...."
Who writes these songs, anyway?

Sleep is something you give up in exchange for the joy of motherhood.

When your baby wakes you up
at night, just be happy he is
not a teen out with your car.
(No, don't think about that!)

Your baby is fresh from
God's heart to yours.

There is no thunder as
loud as your baby
bawling at midnight.

An infant's burp is somehow as endearing as a gentleman's bow.

One of baby's first talents
is to poke mom in the
eye with her tiny finger.
It would appear to
be effortless.

*You created my inmost being;
you knit me together in my
mother's womb. I praise you
because I am fearfully and
wonderfully made;
your works are wonderful,
I know that full well.*

PSALM 139:13-14 NIV

After the first few nights
of being home with your
infant, you will experience
the senility of old age.
This is caused by lack of sleep.

The first employment
of a baby is to train
her parents.

Placing a baby in his carrier seat aboard the clothes dryer will often lull him to sleep, but don't be surprised if you find a sleep-deprived daddy already there.

Don't let it frighten you, but from the day your baby is born, you have only thirteen years to prepare yourself for being the mom of a teenager.

Chocolate always helps!

Never be harsh with baby.
He is only trying to be cute, right?

A baby's hands curled together while he sleeps is one of the most wonderful sights in the world.

A baby teaches her parents
how to laugh and play again.

When the baby is asleep in church,
he takes after Daddy's side of the family.
When the baby is squalling at 2 a.m.,
she takes after Mom's.

If evolution really works,
how come mothers only
have two hands?

Milton Berle

There is a "tired" a mom of a new baby experiences that compares easily to the exhaustion that a mountain climber feels on Mt. Everest.

Eat right, drink plenty of water, and get eight hours of deep sleep every night. (Yeah, right!)

Dogs vs. babies: dogs drool, and they are not half as cute as human babies.

Babies are wonderful
from a distance and sweeter
yet up close.

"A baby is a blessing"
was first whispered
during naptime.

Never underestimate the power
of an infant's first gurgling
laugh on a daddy's heart.

Tired? Don't worry,
you'll get used to it.

Post-pregnancy perk: Did you ever imagine you'd be thrilled to get back into a size large?

How is it that a baby's
breathing is so soft you
can barely perceive it,
yet he can yell loud enough to
be heard in the next county?

*All thy children shall be taught
of the Lord; and great shall be
the peace of thy children.*

ISAIAH 54:13 KJV

Why are children so
adverse to naps when
you long for one?

The newfangled baby play
mat with mobiles looks
like so much fun,
but don't try it out or
you could get stuck—
and that's when someone
will knock at the door.

Remember when your living room had furniture instead of swings, playpens, bouncers, carriers, and high chairs?

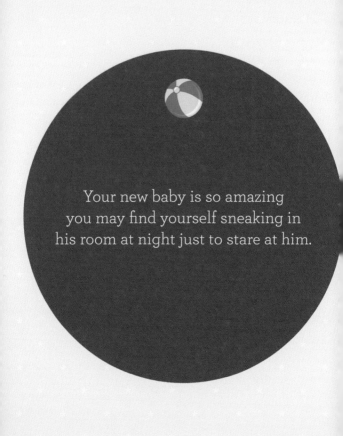

Your new baby is so amazing
you may find yourself sneaking in
his room at night just to stare at him.

Once your baby is born,
you can put him down
sometimes—or can you?

How pathetic is it to be so slap-silly
in love with a little person?

A baby ties big tangled
knots in apron strings.
It will be years full of happy
days before you'll have
to untie them.

Why is a baby's belch funny
when a ten-year-old's is not?

The introduction of a baby to the
family changes the alphabet—
no more ZZZZs.

Even when freshly washed and
relieved of all obvious confections,
children tend to be sticky.

FRAN LEBOWITZ

There is a reason why
a baby's first "talk" is
usually a shortened form
of the word "gooey."

When your child brings you his own clean diaper and informs you he needs a change of upholstery, it is time to start potty training.

There is no more impossible task than to lay a sleeping baby down without waking him.

Babies are irresistible
smidgens of humanity.

How could anything so
infinitely cute not be a puppy?

A baby's cooing can best
any choir's signature piece.

Waiting for baby to finally sleep so you can relax and read will unfortunately put you to sleep also.

Every minute seems long to a too-tired mama, but the years pass like rockets. Enjoy the weary minutes.

*He gives children to the
woman who has none and
makes her a happy mother.*

PSALM 113:9 NCV

Sleeping like a baby sounds good,
but that would be in short snatches
and lightly enough that a whisper
wakens you.

"Goo-goos" and "ga-gas"
are a foreign language
only to the woman who
never held a baby.

When teaching your baby to eat strained veggies, wear green so the spray won't show.

Happy marriage hint:
Always take the plastic cups,
ducks, and boats out of the
bathtub before Daddy's turn.

Toting a child around
on your hip will
make everybody else
look lopsided.

When the baby cries and fusses, everybody works to console him. Wouldn't it be nice if people jumped when Mom whimpered?

Ever wonder why a
fifty-pound diaper bag
seems to have every
baby-care item you
need except for a diaper?

One of the important skills
for motherhood is that of
mopping up spills.

Remember when the thing that worried you most was all the women patting you and saying, "Don't worry"?

People who say they sleep like a baby usually don't have one.

LEO J. BURKE

Bonding with the baby
is what you get Daddy
to do so you can rest.

Infants and teenage girls usually change clothes at least three times before you get out the door.

Binkies are one of the greatest inventions known to womankind.

With a new baby in the house,
sometimes it's Mama who needs
the blankie and the pacifier!

Most of the decorations
in the nursery are
for Mommy.

With the first baby,
Mama throws away a pacifier
that falls on the floor;
with the second, she rinses it
off; for all subsequent babies,
she wipes it on her sleeve.

Ribbons, bows, and tiny shoes
on sweet toes; babies are treasures.

A baby is one of those blessings
God uses to teach us who's in
charge of the universe.

Baby foods must be
chosen with care since
Mom will get to smell, taste,
and clean up more of it than
she gets Junior to swallow.
(Note: Skip anything green.)

A mother learns fast to
give unconditional love with
her baby as the teacher.

I don't know whether they should say "You have a baby" or "The baby has you."

Unknown

If your baby's beautiful and perfect, never cries or fusses, sleeps on schedule and burps on demand, an angel all the time, you're the grandma.

UNKNOWN